JESUS
IS BORN

To Meleah, with much love

Sherrie Johnson

To my wife, LeLe, for her love and patience

Tyler Lybbert

Printed in Mexico.

10 9 8 7 6 5 4 3

ISBN 0-87579-856-X

Designed by Craig Geertsen.

JESUS IS BORN

WRITTEN BY
SHERRIE JOHNSON

ILLUSTRATED BY
TYLER LYBBERT

DESERET BOOK COMPANY
SALT LAKE CITY, UTAH

Samuel had prophesied that in five years Jesus would be born to save all those who believed in Him. He told the Nephites that they would know when the time had come because there would be a day and a night and a day that would be as one day.

But the five years had come, and there was no night without darkness.

Samuel was a Lamanite prophet.

"Behold, the time is past, and the words of Samuel are not fulfilled," the unbelievers said, beginning to mock the believers. "There will be no Christ. Therefore, your joy and your faith have been in vain!" And thus the unbelievers caused a great uproar throughout the land.

When something is "in vain," it is useless.

The persecution grew so great that the believers were sorrowful. They began to fear that the things which had been spoken might not come to pass.

Finally, the wickedness of the unbelievers became so great that they set apart a day, saying, "If by this time the sign has not been given, we will put to death all those who believe."

When the prophet Nephi heard of these wicked plans, he was exceedingly sorrowful. He went out and bowed himself upon the earth and cried mightily to God. He prayed for his people who were about to be destroyed because of their faith in Jesus Christ.

This Nephi is the son of Nephi who was the son of Helaman.

All day Nephi prayed unto the Lord until finally the voice of the Lord came to him, saying, "Lift up your head and be of good cheer; for behold, the time is at hand, and on this night shall the sign be given, and on the morrow come I into the world."

That night the sun went down,
but the earth did not get dark.

Many who had not believed the prophecies were overcome by fear and fell to the earth as if they were dead. They knew that their great plan of destruction against the believers had been frustrated.

All the people upon the face of the whole earth, from the west to the east, in the land north and in the land south, were so exceedingly astonished that they fell to the earth. And they began to fear because of their iniquity and their unbelief.

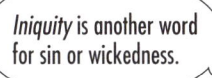
Iniquity is another word for sin or wickedness.

All that night there was no darkness. But in the morning the sun did rise according to its proper order. And all the believers rejoiced, for they knew that this was the day the Lord would be born.

That night a new star appeared
in the sky. Thus were all the words
of the prophets fulfilled.

But Satan sent forth lyings among the people. He tried to make them think that the miracles were because of the tricks of men. Yet most of the people believed the truth and were converted unto the Lord.

Thus Nephi went forth among the people, teaching and baptizing. And the people began again to have peace in the land.

But the peace did not last long. Soon, the Gadianton robbers, who dwelt in the mountains, began to infest the land. They began to steal and to murder. Many of the Nephites and the children of the Lamanites were led away by the lying and the flattering words of the Gadianton robbers.

It was not long before the more part of the people began to forget the signs and wonders of Christ's birth. They began to be less and less astonished by the miracles they had seen and to be hard in their hearts and blind in their minds.

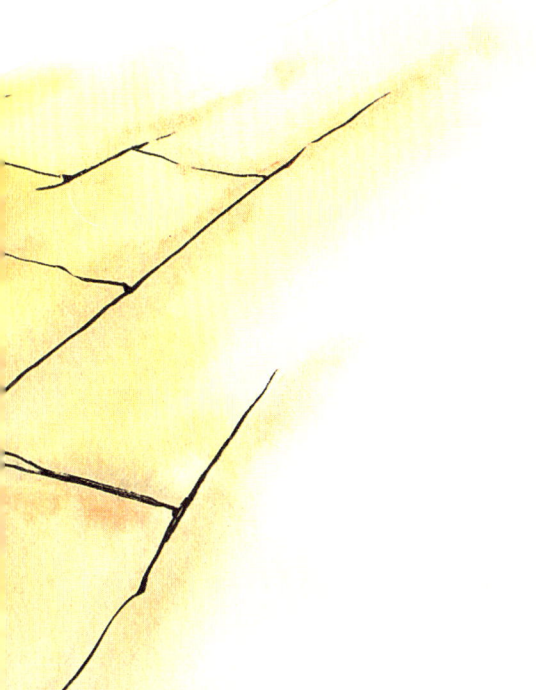

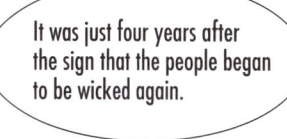

It was just four years after the sign that the people began to be wicked again.

But Nephi could not be deceived. He and the believers knew that the Savior had been born. They knew that the prophecies of Samuel the Lamanite had been fulfilled. They knew that, no matter what the unbelievers said or did, Jesus Christ had been born into the world and that he would atone for the sins of all those who believed in Him.

Atone means to make up for all sin or error.

If you want to read this story in the Book of Mormon, look in 3 Nephi, chapters 1 to 2.